The Polyamorous Relationship

Discover What It Is, How It Works, and Whether or Not It's Right for You

by Peter Landry

Table of Contents

Introduction 1

Chapter 1: Considering a Polyamorous Relationship?
.... 11

Chapter 2: Swinging with Swingers 15

Chapter 3: Understanding Polyfidelity (or Polyexclusivity) 25

Chapter 4: Getting to Know Polyamory and Open Relationships 31

Chapter 5: Deciding Whether or Not It's for You .. 35

Chapter 6: How to Handle a Polyamorous Relationship 39

Conclusion 43

Introduction

My maternal great grandmother was a remarkable woman. I called her Tàipó. She was one of the few Chinese women who were able to enter the US in the early 20th century, skirting the Chinese Exclusionary Laws. Then again, she and my great grandfather didn't come in as ordinary laborers, but as traders.

I remember finding her feet odd, as a child. They were always wrapped, never bare, and no bigger than mine when I was maybe five (the age when I first realized hers were unusual). Her feet were bound, you see. "Lotus feet," as the Chinese say.

When she was four, her toes were broken and forced into the soles of her feet. Then the arch of her foot was broken and forced against her heels. They thought it beautiful at the time, especially since it forced women to walk in tiny, dainty steps. You can't get any more traditional, conservative, and old school than that by Chinese standards.

Since it required daily maintenance to prevent infection and gangrene, she needed a servant to tend to them, so yes, she also arrived in America with a maid servant. There was no way she could do manual labor, so it was a mark of status among highborn women till the Communists finally put a stop to it.

There was also my great grand aunt who lived with my great grandparents. "Gūmā," we used to call her; and yes, she too had lotus feet. For years, I thought she was my Tàipó's much younger sister, till I was finally told the story—Gūmā was my great grandfather's concubine. My Tàipó bought (yes bought) Gūmā for him when my great grand aunt was only 15 years old.

I was aghast, "Why would you do such a thing, Tàipó!?"

I remember seeing my mother, my grandmother, and Gūmā all smirking from the corner of my eye, but I couldn't take my eyes off of my Tàipó. It was as if she'd transmogrified from this tiny woman whom I had always known and loved into something monstrous.

"Because he was too horny, ah!?" was her startling reply. "I couldn't take it anymore, ah! So I bought her," she pointed a delicate finger at Gūmā.

The women shrieked in laughter as I stood there with my jaw on the floor.

I turned toward my great grand aunt in shocked sympathy, "H-h-how do you feel about all this, Gūmā?"

She smiled at me kindly and looked at the household altar. Near center stage was the black-and-white death portrait of my great grandfather who had died years before.

"It was a great life," was her reply.

Then she and my Tàipó exchanged a look I've never forgotten—it was radiant, it was loving, and it was absolutely joyful, "Yes, yes," my Tàipó nodded, still chuckling. "Best buy I ever made, ah?"

I apologize for such a long intro, but I wanted you to know where I'm coming from.

"Poly" comes from the Greek word meaning "many," while "amor" comes from the Latin word for "love." We understand polyamorous to mean having a romantic and/or sexual relationship with more than

3

one partner—ideally with the consent of both (as was the case with my great grandparents and great grand aunt's ménage à trois).

Technically speaking, open relationships and swinging are considered to be polyamorous. But my own personal experience has shown that they do not necessarily mean the same thing.

In case you're wondering, "open relationships" refers to (usually unmarried) couples who consider themselves to be committed to each other. That commitment, however, does not bar them from having sexual and emotional relationships with others. Ideally, both know what the other is doing and both approve.

Swingers are usually (but not always) married people who swap spouses. These usually meet up with other (usually) married swingers for friendship, support, and sex—though not necessarily foursomes (or more). Swinging is both a lifestyle and a subculture, complete with its own codes and set of rules which vary from place to place.

As you can see, polyamorous relationships cover quite a large gamut of pairings. Polyamory (or poly for short), is simply an umbrella term for any couple (married or otherwise) who do not limit their emotional and sexual needs to each other.

My great grandparents' relationship was not an open one, nor did they engage in the swinging lifestyle (to my knowledge, at least). They did so to meet a need: the Chinese desire to have as many children (preferably sons) as possible.

It was also the result of my Tàipó's desire to stop having sex. She had already produced several American-born children and didn't want to go through any more pregnancies.

The point I'm trying to make is this: there are many reasons to engage in a polyamorous relationship. While we may think of it as something modern, many ancient civilizations have practiced it for a long time and still do.

Islamic law, for example, allows a man to have more than one wife. Technically, that's not polyamory; it's polygamy. In Nepal, some tribes practice polyandry— the opposite, where one woman is married to several husbands.

Whatever your reasons are for considering a polyamorous relationship, understand that it's a vast and complicated topic. In this book, I'm going to do my best to cover everything you'll need to consider in deciding whether or not this is the lifestyle for you.

© Copyright 2015 by Miafn LLC - All rights reserved.

This document is geared towards providing reliable information in regards to the topic and issue covered. The publication is sold with the idea that the publisher is not required to render accounting, officially permitted, or otherwise, qualified services. If advice is necessary, legal or professional, a practiced individual in the profession should be ordered.

- From a Declaration of Principles which was accepted and approved equally by a Committee of the American Bar Association and a Committee of Publishers and Associations.

In no way is it legal to reproduce, duplicate, or transmit any part of this document in either electronic means or in printed format. Recording of this publication is strictly prohibited and any storage of this document is not allowed unless with written permission from the publisher. All rights reserved.

The information provided herein is stated to be truthful and consistent, in that any liability, in terms of inattention or otherwise, by any usage or abuse of any policies, processes, or directions contained within is solely and completely the responsibility of the recipient reader. Under no circumstances will any legal responsibility or blame be held against the publisher for any reparation, damages, or monetary loss due to the information herein, either directly or indirectly.

Respective authors own all copyrights not held by the publisher.

The information herein is offered for informational purposes solely, and is universal as so. The presentation of the information is without contract or any type of guarantee assurance.

The trademarks that are used are without any consent, and the publication of the trademark is without permission or backing by the trademark owner. All trademarks and brands within this book are for clarifying purposes only and are the owned by the owners themselves, not affiliated with this document.

Chapter 1: Considering a Polyamorous Relationship?

I'm going to assume that you're probably a lot like I used to be.

By this I mean that you're used to the traditional (Western Christian) view of what a committed relationship looks like. When I say "committed relationship," I am referring to both gay and straight ones, as well as to married and unmarried (but extremely serious and long term) ones.

In this worldview, a committed relationship is something that exists exclusively between two people. Period.

It's like a contract. If one partner has sex with someone else, then they have violated that contract. They've cheated, gone AWOL, became unfaithful, betrayed the other, have stabbed their partner in the back, and so on.

The fact that you're even reading this, however, tells me that you've begun to "think outside the box," shall we say? As such, you're wondering:

1. What to do about it

2. If it's the right thing to do or not

No one but you can answer those questions, of course. But if you're reading this, then the reason you're thinking outside the box is because you're facing one (or more) of five possibilities:

1. You're flirting with the idea of a polyamorous relationship

2. Your partner is flirting with the idea of one

3. You're already in a polyamorous relationship and want your partner in on it

4. Your partner wants to explore and you're not sure how you feel about it

5. You both want to get into it but aren't sure how to start

I can't tell you if it's the right thing to do or what to do about it. I'm neither your confessor nor your psychologist; nor do I have any desire to be either. But I can tell you some things about polyamory, and the rest is up to you. I'll provide an overview of the different types of polyamorous relationships out there.

I want to make it clear that I'm not an expert on the matter. But after my Tàipó and Gūmā opened my mind to the fact that there are other types of genuinely loving relationships out there, I began to look deeper into the topic. The more I looked, the more I met others who were in such unconventional relationships, and the more I began to understand.

I therefore believe that I'm in a unique position to address those five possibilities and in that order. Hopefully, it'll also help you to understand, and in doing so, help you in whatever you decide to do. At the very least, I hope I can get you through issue number four—especially if you're not too happy about it.

Chapter 2: Swinging with Swingers

I'd like to begin with this one because it divides the poly community.

As I've already mentioned, polyamory is a vast topic. So far, my Word program refuses to underline the variations of that term in red. This means that while the people who work at Microsoft may be geeks, some of them lead very interesting lives.

When it comes to the swinging lifestyle, however, quite a number of poly types shake their heads.

The term "swinging" goes back to the 1960s. The invention of the pill made the sexual revolution possible. Back then, it was called "wife swapping," though the more gender sensitive preferred term is "partner sharing." Since the women also had a say in the matter, however, they finally coined the phrase "swinging" and "swingers" to make it more politically correct and gender neutral.

The reason some poly types shake their heads is because swinging is particularly focused on sex. I know how strange that sounds, but I promise that bit will be covered in greater detail later.

Swingers swap their spouses or have foursomes with other couples for several reasons:

1. To spice up their marriage

2. To maintain their partnership while overcoming the humdrum of sexual routine

3. Out of curiosity

4. As a way of increasing their social circle

Swingers are generally happy in their marriages and with their partners. There are even those who swear that:

1. The swinging lifestyle saved their marriages

2. Deepened their relationship with their spouse

3. Introduced a greater depth of intimacy into their marital beds

In 2005, Fox News aired a special investigative report hosted by John Stossel about the swinger's lifestyle. In it, the swingers told Stossel that they felt more secure with their marriages, as a result.

For this to happen, however, there are three rules that all swingers agree on:

1. That both spouses accept the idea

2. That both enter a swing club or party together, never separately, to ensure that both are on board and know what the other is doing

3. That everyone at swing clubs and parties practice safe sex—many such venues even provide condoms

Going back to that TV program, the swingers felt that by being honest with their spouses, they weren't cheating on them. When the couples were asked if they were afraid of being left for another wo/man, the answer shocked the host. According to the interviewees, they joined swingers clubs to share their spouses, not replace them.

SO HOW DO YOU START?

Find yourself a swingers club or party online

Most who start out take pains to choose a venue as far from where they live as possible. Do note, however, that newbie swingers in your area will probably do the same, so your chances of bumping into people you know is high—especially if you live in a rural area. Who knows, you might even meet a couple who works for Microsoft!

As a general rule of thumb, clubs have their regulars who understand your first time jitters because they've been there before. Most are happy to guide you through the process while respecting your boundaries.

Parties, on the other hand, are filled with many first timers who are as nervous as you are about the whole thing. Fortunately, those parties are also hosted by pros who are usually very accommodating and helpful.

Partnering

Couples who've been doing this for a long time are fine with going to a party or club together, picking up partners, and going their separate ways to meet up back home later. But we won't cover that here since you're not yet there, are you?

This is the nerve-wracking part: finding the chosen couple. Do note that as you judge the others, so they'll be judging you. But the thing about swinging, especially for first timers is that yours isn't the final decision. Your partner must make that decision with you because you're going for a foursome (at the very least).

If you settle for an experienced couple, then let them take the lead. That said, be sure to set your boundaries and stick to them. What works for them might not work for you, especially in the beginning. Swingers are not sex fiends, they're simply people who want to experiment and broaden their horizons with their partners in tow.

But if you settle on fellow newbies, aah… that's where it gets tricky.

Soft swinging (or soft swap)

This is how newbies dip their toes gently into the water. It also applies to experienced couples who are meeting for the first time and want to give the other a test drive.

For the former, it involves you having sex with your spouse, while the other couple also have sex—but with distance between you. That distance could be in the next room across the hall with both your doors open, or on a separate bed where you can see the other but not touch, or better yet—on the same large bed (or carpet).

Take the initiative

The last one (having sex on the same bed) is the best option because it encourages the illusion of distance and boundaries while leaving room for more. No one is expecting to hook up with a couple who has a Master's Degree in the Kama Sutra. Nor is this book devoted to the art of voyeurism.

First timers rarely find themselves keeping the other's contact details because they're usually too nervous and act accordingly. The important thing, however, is to take the plunge. If they won't, then you must.

Think of it as your first time with your (original) partner, but before you do, remember the boundary thing again. Some men don't like being touched by other men (ditto with women). If you want to try swinging to explore your gay side, make that *very clear* before all four of you hop into the car for the drive home. If that's not your thing, but the other couple wants it, then keep looking.

Simply reach out and touch, but avoid sensitive spots like breasts and genitalia. Ditto with kissing. Begin with something less sensitive, like the legs, arms, or back. As you do, pay very careful attention to how the one you touch reacts, as well as to how their (original) partner does. If they flinch, back off.

In soft swinging, there is no genital sex. Some argue as to whether or not a hand job qualifies as a soft swap, but I won't bother with that here.

Hard swinging (or hard swap)

Some couples take a while to warm up, while others are ready to get into the swing of things all the way.

Only make your way to the genital area when both are completely relaxed. Hard swinging is where full-on genital sex happens.

As a newbie, you might want to wait till you find a couple you "click" with before getting to this point. And when I say "you," I of course mean "you and your partner."

On the topic of boundaries

I really can't emphasize this point enough. The vast majority of swingers set very specific boundaries and make them extremely clear during the initial meeting.

Strange as it may sound, kissing is one of them. Not all couples set that boundary, of course but many do. Since swingers are usually married, they like to think that they're keeping back something very special that they reserve only for their original partners.

Orgasm is yet another tricky bit. Some men are fine with another man fucking their wife, but they're not ok with them coming inside her—even when the other guy is wearing a condom. Still others have no problems with their wife giving another man a blowjob, so long as he doesn't cum in her mouth or on her face.

Interestingly enough, this applies to some gay couples, as well. Ditto with the kissing part.

Chapter 3: Understanding Polyfidelity (or Polyexclusivity)

Some call it "group marriage," which is impossible, of course, since no government (yet) recognizes such a thing. Still others prefer the term "tribes."

It's sort of like polygamy and polyandry and swinging, but more complicated. In polyfidelity, you can have all manner of pairings (guy-guy, girl-girl, and guy-girl) which allow for group sex. But there's a catch. You can only have sex within your closed circle.

Having sex outside that group is cheating. For this to work, everyone in that tribe obviously has to get along.

The advantage of this is that so long as everyone sticks to the rules, and so long as they all have a medical check-up before signing on, they can have multiple partners without the risk of contracting an STD.

There are many variations of polyfidelity. The Kerista Village movement in San Francisco tried it out from 1971 to 1991, maintaining a purely heterosexual community. They shared resources and property, and lived like a large family before they split up. Some still remain "married," but their numbers are now smaller.

Geometric Relationships

There are various types of polyexclusive relationships. The most common one is called a "geometric relationship." In some cases, these are essentially modern terms for polygamy or polyandry.

Triads

This usually involves a legally married couple who live with a third person. Often, that third person is considered to be a spouse (as was the case with my Gūmā) and shares the man's bed. I'm told that some Mormon families who still practice polygamy (despite the ban on it), prefer this term to avoid problems with federal law.

Vs

Also spelled "vee," this again involves three people, but they don't have to be married. In a V relationship, one is the hinge, while the other two are adjuncts. A typical V pairing involves a man and two women, or one woman and two men. Vs are usually temporary because two members have a stronger bond and were already together when the third person entered the relationship.

Quads

Quads usually involve two legally married couples who live together as a single family unit. Not only do they share a home and all the responsibility that entails (including rearing children), but they also share each other's beds. While most quads are heterosexual couples, other sexual pairings also exist.

Ns

Ns again involve two couples (not necessarily married and not necessarily heterosexual), but it's complicated, so please bear with my diagram. In an N relationship, you have Person A who's with Person B, and Person C who's with Person D. With me so far?

The thing is, Person A has strong feelings for Person C, which are reciprocated. Since Person B wants their partner to be happy, ditto with person D, they're fine with A and C getting it on. In some cases, B and D get it on, as well.

What makes Ns different from Quads is that A has no interest in D (at least not in that way) and B has no interest in C.

Mono-Poly (or mono/poly)

This is the one my Tàipó had. After having eleven children, she was fed up with sex. Since my great grandfather went on to sire five more children with Gūmā, it was clear he wasn't fed up with it yet. In fact, family rumor has it that we have far more blood relatives in California than we know about.

Mono-Polies are relationships where one partner has no interest in playing around, but their partner does. What makes mono-polies different from marriages or partnerships with a cheating other half? In a mono-poly, the monogamous one knows about and is fine with the partner who likes to play around.

THERE'S MORE…

Quite a lot, actually, but I feel those about cover the gamut. The rest are mere variations of those I've already cited.

The point I've tried to make in this section is that fidelity, faithfulness, and loyalty does not necessarily have to be limited to one other person. In some cultures, polygamy and polyandry are the norm. This doesn't mean those cultures are peopled by sexually depraved beings. Only that they have different standards.

Some define "traditional" marriage as a bond between one man and one woman only. Others suggest that without this exclusive pairing, chaos will ensue. Most who spout such nonsense have never traveled farther than the nearest mall or 7-11. Or if they have, they never strayed beyond the guided tours.

Ours is a diverse world with equally diverse concepts of what qualifies as "traditional," "right," "normal," and "proper." The same certainly applies to the concept of relationships, as well as to what constitutes fidelity.

Chapter 4: Getting to Know Polyamory and Open Relationships

"Amor," love, is the key word here, and explains why some who embrace the poly lifestyle look down on swingers. Poly people, like monogamists, also seek intimacy, companionship, and love. Yes, love. It's just that they don't equate love with the physical act of sex. You might want to read that last line again.

Polyamorous people are capable of romantic sentiments and can be fiercely loyal to their partners. They can stand by them no matter what and sacrifice a lot for the good of their mates. They can also have their hearts broken.

But they also see the sexual act as both a biological function as well as a human need. As such, the fulfillment of that need is not seen as a compromise of what they feel toward their partners.

To poly people, sexual commitment to just one person is suffocating. It's like being told they can't talk to someone else, hang out with their old friends, talk or look at someone of the opposite sex (or the same in the case of gays and lesbians), can't touch another human being, can't smile at someone, can't befriend another, etc.

They don't believe that having sex with others in any way, shape, or form mitigates their love for their partner. This is the same argument that swingers espouse—which makes the polyamorous rather hypocritical in their disdain, don't you think?

Some even go so far as to suggest that polyamory is a sexual orientation, like being straight, gay, or bi. There is actually an international polyamorous movement, and their values are as follows:

1) Faith and loyalty are about who you commit to and wish to spend the rest of your life with. A polyamorous person is therefore open about their sexual needs with their partner and does not engage in secret relationships. When sleeping with others, they take great care to practice safe sex so as not to infect themselves and their partners.

2) Negotiation and agreement are about compromise and understanding that not all are comfortable with open relationships. Polyamorous people therefore agree to certain conditions with their partners (especially those who are monogamous). This includes letting their primary partners know about their other relationships.

3) Boundaries are important because even the polyamorous see the value of living and acting within a specific framework. The practice of safe sex is part of those boundaries.

4) Respect and dignity means that the polyamorous respect the dignity of all their partners, sexual and otherwise. It also means that they respect gender and sexual preferences regardless of their own sexual orientation.

5) Non-possessiveness is the view that no one can own another, nor impose unrealistic or unreasonable demands that limit them. Jealousy and possessiveness are therefore seen as responses to be explored and understood, and if possible, avoided.

Chapter 5: Deciding Whether or Not It's for You

I've explained the many types of polyamorous relationships out there that you and/or your partner can explore if you're interested. What I'd now like to do is address the awkward situation in which everything I've described just isn't your thing. Unfortunately, your partner feels otherwise.

Assuming you haven't already dumped him or her, and assuming you still want to stay together, there are a few things you have to bear in mind. The first thing I'd like to reiterate is what I said in the last chapter:

Polyamorists don't equate love with the physical act of sex. That's the key thing right there.

What I'm trying to say is that: (1) unless your partner dumps you for someone else, and (2) assuming they say they love you and mean it, it's just that they want to have sex with others, then (3) what you've got there is a polyamorous person.

They actually do love you. Just not in the way you may approve of. In other words, it's not about you. It's not a rejection of you, it's not because you've suddenly gained weight, or that you snore, or that they don't like your family, etc. For that, they'd dump you outright.

No, no. It's about them. Them. Your partner isn't attacking or criticizing you. They're being honest with you because they don't want to do anything sneaky behind your back. The fact that they're even telling you about it is because they still want you in their lives.

Nor does it necessarily mean you suck in bed. You could have a Doctorate degree in the Kama Sutra, but it still doesn't matter. I repeat—it's not about you.

Monogamists are happy with one person, the polyamorous are not. When a polyamorous person falls in love, the romantic desire for a special connection with others doesn't shut off as it does with monogamists.

So when they say that one person doesn't satisfy their needs, it doesn't mean they're spoiled brats who want every desire met, no matter how minor it is. It simply means that their desire for that special intimacy with another cannot be met by one person alone.

It's like being gay or straight. I know that comes across as shocking to you, an attempt to justify cheating lovers, but it's not. I won't get into the science, but some suggest that the brains of genuinely monogamous people are different from genuinely polyamorous people.

That said, some people are just assholes. Cheating lovers and polyamorous people are not the same thing. The former just can't keep their pants or skirts on, regardless of the consequences to themselves and to others. The latter, on the other hand, is really looking for a romantic connection… again and again and again.

Sometimes, the best option is to just let them go or to walk away.

Chapter 6: How to Handle a Polyamorous Relationship

It's possible you've outgrown your current relationship and want to move on, but can't or won't for whatever reason. It's even possible that you still love your partner, but that sexual zing is no longer there. Finally, consider the possibility that your partner feels either of the above regarding you. Whatever the case, you owe each other the truth.

I want to make it very clear that while polyamory has saved some relationships, it has destroyed many others. It takes a certain kind of mindset to be able to share one's partner both on a sexual as well as on an emotional level.

If polyamory is indeed a sexual orientation, that could explain it. In an ideal world, the polyamorists stick to their kind and the monogamists stay together. Unfortunately, our world has never been ideal, now has it?

If you choose to stay in a relationship with a polyamorous person, know it won't be easy. Sometimes, your best option is to just walk away. And if you want to experiment with polyamory, understand that you can't always have your cake and eat it. Your original partner might not be able to take it, so be ready to let go.

But if you decide to give it a shot, you need to consider three important things:

Understand what kind of polyamorous relationship you're getting into. I've described the various kinds of pairings and the rules that generally govern them. Open relationships and swinging mean you and/or your partner have sex with others, but there's no emotional commitment to those others. This is the ideal for those starting out.

If you're getting into a polyfidelic relationship, first see how those in the circle relate to each other. They may be great when you're looking at them from the outside, but another matter when you're on the inside looking out.

Be flexible but know your boundaries, something you should do in a monogamous relationship, as well. The first key lies in understanding that your partner's motives and behavior are not always about you. The other key lies in them understanding the same thing.

Nevertheless, you do have a right to have your needs respected. If your open relationship ends up with your partner wanting to move a third person in and you're not fine with that, get ready to either walk away or adapt to that new other.

Don't assume the problem has to do with polyamory. When problems arise, it's easy to blame the unconventional relationship as the cause. This isn't fair, since monogamous relationships have their own problems, too. It's best to deal with the problem specifically, and don't assume it's because of the relationship.

Of course if polyamory is indeed the problem, then that's another matter entirely. How you deal with that issue is up to you.

Conclusion

Tàipó and Gūmā lived generally happy and fulfilling lives because they grew up in a different world with a different mindset and different expectations. Polyamory is like that for the vast majority of us today—different.

That does not make it wrong or perverse.

Should you decide to experiment with polyamory, understand that it has both positive and negative aspects. In the end, how happy or not you become depends on you, not your sexual orientation or relationship choices.

That said, you should also understand that every decision you make comes with consequences—both good and bad. Whatever you decide, I wish you happiness and fulfillment.

Finally, I'd like to thank you for purchasing this book! If you enjoyed it or found it helpful, I'd greatly appreciate it if you'd take a moment to leave a review on Amazon. Thank you!

Printed in Poland
by Amazon Fulfillment
Poland Sp. z o.o., Wrocław